# The Staffordshire Larder

### A Definitive Guide To

## Wild Foods In Staffordshires, Cities, Towns, Country Parks, and Countryside

# I'll Never Go Hungry In Staffordshire

As I walk from my terraced house in Leek, heading towards town, I pass plants growing on the side of the pavement: one, two, three, four different species of what many know as weeds but to me are the makings of a perfect dish. Then I ask myself, "Why am I going to the shops to buy my salad?" At least I won't look strange carrying food in a packet.

(Author Pete Bridgwood)

Staffordshire is unique; its complexity matches anywhere else in the United Kingdom, from the barren Moorlands of the Peak District to the back gardens in the city centre of Stoke-on-Trent. To many they are two worlds apart, but in reality both have their own story of the relationship they share along with all the other streets, gardens, country parks, and parts of countryside in Staffordshire – its free food.

This guide aims to open one's eyes to what is to be had in this county of secret and delight.

## About The Author

Pete Bridgwood began his life growing up on the outdoors. From a very young age Pete was encouraged to take advantage of the benefits that the outdoors offers. Living in Leek, Staffordshire, Pete is a stone's through away from the Peak District – to him his true love. He has benefited from the many rewards the Peak District holds. Pete is a qualified rock climbing and mountain Instructor and is the chief instructor of Freeworld Adventures, which provides courses in surviving in the wild, all over the country. Pete has had the privilege to travel extensively throughout Staffordshire, gaining knowledge as he moves about foods that can be eaten from the wild, and he now wants to share his knowledge with you.

# Acknowledgements

Until its publishing, the Staffordshire Larder was a bit of a secret. The author quietly went about his daily research, but unknowingly, help was given. I would like to pay particular thanks to my dear wife, Grace, my family, and Grace's family for supporting me in my outdoor way of life and understanding my need for adventure.

# **Contents**

# Introduction

For thousands of years, Homo sapiens have hunted and gathered on our fragile planet. Each country, each county, each area, each hill, each species has a fine balance in which man has been a part of. Only in recent times has the demand for food grown with the expansion of civilisation, and at the same time, our demand for convenience has let us forget the natural resources that our also at hand.

The United Kingdom has hundreds of plant and animal species that all play their part in the food chain. Each area, whether it is coastal, mountainous, hill, or moorland, has a variety of species that are unique to its landscapes.

Staffordshire is like any other unique landscape. From its northern tip of the Moorlands and bleak peat bog landscapes, where the Staffordshire Roaches stand guard, to the many rolling hills, which give way to meadows, hills, villages, towns, cities, parks, and gardens – all gently hold their secrets.

This guide aims to unearth the many natural delights that are available all through the year, in all parts of Staffordshire. From the amateur to the field guide specialist, this book will assist all those who want to learn more, whether a resident of Staffordshire or not.

I invite you all to open your eyes to The Staffordshire Larder.

# How To Use This Book

This guide is unique. Unlike many, it is specified to within Staffordshire. Many of the plants and animals may be common and can be found in many other parts of the United Kingdom. Understandably the professional botanist or wise countryman may feel short-changed by this guide, because it purposely avoids many species of plant and fungi. However, this reason is justified to suit the many that have no or very little knowledge of wild foods.

A vast range of wild foods look, smell, or taste similar. Edible and poisonous species which do look the same share the same patches of ground. This sometimes may be a disadvantage to the amateur, as it encourages them to avoid the edible species for the taking. This guide has simplified the searching for the reader, so there is little confusion.

The guide's size makes it a handy complement which can fit in the rucksack for all those who want to access its contents. From a guide instructing a group to a family day out, this guide will assist your curiosity wherever you are in Staffordshire.

The pictures show a close-up of the wild food; some are even closer shots, for the reader to be able to distinguish certain parts of the species. All species are given their common name(s), followed by the Latin equivalent and height underneath, with the time of year to find them.

The text covers a brief description of habitat, distribution, and growth characteristics, followed by a "what to do" or a "what to use for" box underneath for the reader to be able to pick, use, and preserve the species for its use.

10

---

**EXPLANATION OF THE SYMBOLS**

☺ = Excellent eating

☺ = Quite good eating

☹ = Edible, but not great eating

---

# Safety

The Staffordshire Larder simplifies the species to make them easy to identify. Using the book allows the reader to compare photos from the guide to the species in the field. However, it is not possible that all readers will be able to make a positive identification 100 per cent of the time; in this case avoidance is the best option. If you are ever in doubt, do not eat what you have found. If you are concerned or wish to know more, expert advice should be sought. If you have eaten a species which you suspect could have been poisonous, seek medical advice immediately, and if possible, bring a sample of what you have eaten along with a description of where you found it and what you thought the species was.

This guide has made accurate descriptions which it believes to be true. Neither the author nor the publisher accept legal responsibility for any harm caused from advice or techniques given in this guide.

## The Protection Of Species And Habitats

At the time of writing, this guide does not identify any species that is either rare or in danger of extinction. However, this does not give the reader the right to take many numbers of the same species, especially from the same place. When taking species, act responsibly; only take one or two samples from one location.

There are pieces of legislation that protect species in the United Kingdom. Please respect these and act responsibly when foraging or hunting for wild foods, to preserve the species as well as future generations to enjoy.

## Plants and Trees

By far the most common and majority of make-up in this guide is that of plants and trees. There are hundreds of plants and trees with many thousands of uses. Later volumes of this series will look at medicinal properties and making items from plant and tree resources from Staffordshire. However, this guide will concentrate on the simple-to-identify plants and trees with little or no preparation before consuming. Complex botanical identification of plants usually consists of identifying the number of petals it has, followed by the colour, structure, flower type, and roots. This guide has simplified this so that common, easy-to-identify plant species can be made. When harvesting plants for consumption, always pick young specimens with fresh growth, unless specified in the guide. Plants become more toxic as they get older, thus becoming unsafe for consumption. Many plant sources can be found alongside roads and in busy, built-up areas. There is no limitation on harvesting these species; however, care and consideration must be made as to whether a species has been exposed to toxins or pollution, or has been used by animals, which can pose a threat to consumption.

Tree identification is not as complex as plant identification; leaf identification, height, roots, and bark can easily be distinguished. However, care must still be taken, as many tree species hold bitter toxins which can poison the body as they mature. Many tree species hold berries which are poisonous and should be avoided unless stated in this guide.

# Fruits And Nuts

Staffordshire is blessed to have a variety of habitats which allow such an array of fruits and nuts to grow. Fruits can vary in shape, size, colour, time of year, and location. Fruits have the advantage of becoming an excellent snack and in some cases can be harvested in great quantities. However, many fruits are toxic and, unless 100 per cent positively identified, should be avoided.

Nearly all nut species within the UK can be eaten. Highly nutritious, they are an excellent food source which should be prized. Nuts usually occur in the late summer and can last through autumn into the winter. Many animals rely on nuts as a food source during the winter, so careful consideration should be made when picking nuts in great quantities.

# Roots And Tubers

Many plants build up stores of carbohydrates within their roots. In some cases roots and tubers can grow to considerable size, which makes them excellent eating. Most roots will build up their stores through the summer for winter months. Autumn is the best time for roots and tubers to be picked. Some can be eaten straight away, but many need to be cooked first.

# Mushrooms

The reader may find that this guide has a limited number of mushrooms identified. This is justified, because mushrooms pose the greatest threat to the amateur. Various types of mushrooms are edible; however, they can produce toxins if not transported, cooked, and sometimes picked correctly. This guide identifies mushroom species which are easily identified, found, and picked. The reader should compare photos of mushrooms from the guide with those in the field.

Mushrooms are a complex organism. The flower which we see is just the start of the matrix root system to which it belongs. There are hundreds of types of mushrooms, growing in various climates, conditions, and habitats. They vary in shape, size, smell, and colour, and they must ALWAYS be 100 per cent positively identified. Under no circumstances should one pick and eat a mushroom straight from the field; always cook it thoroughly first.

When picking mushrooms, use a sharp knife and transport in an airy container (e.g., a basket) because mushrooms develop toxins when transported in carriers or plastic bags.

# Animals

The range of animals in Staffordshire varies massively. From four-legged mammals to legless grubs and fish, there are more protein sources to be found than first thought. Staffordshire has a great larder of animals that can be eaten; some can be found in one's own garden, and some may need hunting.

Game and large prey hunting quite often involves the particular animal species having protection or seasonal hunting rights against it, so it is always advisable that you seek landowner permission or go in a organised party before hunting.

# Preparing, Storing, And Using Your Foods

So you've identified your food, it's been picked, and now it's at home waiting for the next step. So what do you do?

This is where it's important to act quickly; fresh food does not stay fresh for long, and it's a good idea to have a plan for your fresh pickings before it's taken from the wild.

Some foods need immediate attention, particularly fungi, because they rot fast. Here you can decide whether you are going to cook or store it. Below is a list of preparation and preserving methods and ways to store your goods.

## Drying

By far the most effective method for preserving, drying enables the freshness and taste of a food to be retained and can be stored for weeks, months, and even years.

There are two great methods of drying indoors. The first is to thinly slice your foods and put on a baking sheet in a very low-heat oven until drying is complete. Quite often smaller or less moist foods will dry first. The second method is to set up a wire rack or basket above a radiator and place your thinly sliced foods on it; don't forget to turn your radiator on! Alternatively, you can thread string or cotton through the food and hang above the radiator until dried.

If outdoors, it is best to leave items in the heat of the sun, usually hanging in an exposed place using the thread method or wire rack method.

Plants have the benefit of drying out without the use of heat. For best results, tie a small bunch of your plant by the stems and hang until dry, usually a few days to a week.

To store your dried goods, put in an airtight container or food pot. You will know if the food is not dried out properly or moisture has got in, as it will be rotting

## Smoking

Smoking is a fantastic way of dramatically extending the life of a dried food whilst still retaining taste and goodness.

If outdoors, it is possible to either place your food through skewers above a small fire on a makeshift rack, or have it hanging on the end of a stick above a fire (particularly useful for hot smoking fish).

If at home, unless you have an expensive smoker, you could try an alternative method. Place wood chippings or sawdust in a barbeque and light, but do not let it burn through, just smoulder. Have your food on a rack above and then close the lid and wait until cooked. Alternatively, if you want to cold smoke, you will need to create a makeshift smoker, consisting of a barrel where the food hangs, connected at the bottom by some metal piping, which at the entrance your chippings are smouldering. Smoke is forced through the piping and smokes and flavours the food. Just remember to have a lid on!

Store smoked food hanging in a cool place or in an airtight container.

## Pickling

Pickling consists of storing your food in vinegar or oil in an airtight container. It works well for nuts and fungi and some plants, such as onions, tomatoes, or garlic.

## Another way to store

Some foods with hard bodies, for example roots, tubers and some hard fruits, can be stored in a different way. In the past it would have been buried in the ground for winter use, usually in sand, but if you don't fancy this method, an alternative way is to individually wrap your food in a piece of newspaper, place all items in a box and put in a cool place like an outdoor shed or cellar. This method will sometimes preserve your food for months at a time, a good tip for the winter.

# Using your food

Below is a list of simple ways to create dishes for your foods:

- *Sauces* – The best way to use wild foods, especially with mushroom or plants with strong flavour. A simple sauce will usually consist of your wild food being mixed with other ingredients and boiled with water, milk, or cream until it is the desired consistency.

- *Salads* – This is a great way to eat in the field; many small plants can be put together to create an excellent combination.

- *Chutneys* – These work best by combining your wild foods and mixing with vinegar, salt, and a base food (onion is best), along with water and sugar. Simmer all together until a chutney consistency, usually a couple hours.

- *Jams* – A jam is made with fruits, and almost any can be used, but it requires pectin to help the jam set. If you do not bought pectin, a wild alternative can be used from chopped-up crab apples or damsons, both of which contain the enzyme. To make a simple jam, chop your fruit to your consistency, then add a helping of sugar and water and the pectin. Cook on a gentle heat until the sugar is dissolved, then rapidly boil for ten minutes. Jar up for storage.

- *Crumbles* – Once again, these can be made from a sweet ingredient. A fruit base layer will need boiling with a little water and sugar until the required consistency. The crumble itself is made from a measurement of flour, mixed with half its weight in butter and the same in sugar. To make a healthier crumble, reduce the amount of butter and sugar and add a little more flour.

- *Pies* – Weather sweet or savoury, pies are excellent eating. The filling will depend on what you're using, but for a simple pastry base, make up a batch of short crust pastry by mixing a quantity of flour mixed with half its weight in butter and a little water to combine.

- *Infusions* – There are lots of ways to infuse foods. Ones that work well are butter and ice infusions. For butter infusions, finely chop your ingredient and infuse with butter overnight. For ice cubes, plants and flowers work best. Either place straight in an ice cube tub or place in the freezer, or boil your ingredient in water, allow it to cool, and then freeze it. This works particularly well with mints and marigolds.

- *Wines* – A fantastic way to use your wild foods, wines can be made from almost any ingredient. Adding your wild food only gives the wine flavour, as it is possible to create wine from simple base ingredients. To make a simple wine, mix your wild food (e.g., raspberry) with a gallon of water in a bucket and three-quarters bag of sugar. Mix all together, let it cool, and then add yeast. Allow to ferment for a few days to strain into a demijohn and leave for three months. Syphon of into bottles and then leave to mature longer if desired.

- *Spirits and liquors* – There are two ways to do this. Either infuse your wild food with an existing spirit, or mix together a wild fruit which you picked with a generous quantity of sugar and a little yeast. Put in a plastic bottle or similar container and let it ferment itself over a couple months. Release the pressure every couple days.

- *Syrups and cordials* – A fantastic way of using fruits. Mash your fruits to a pulp, mix with a generous helping of sugar and boiling water, and leave to infuse for a few days. Strain and then bottle and use as desired.

15

16

# Plants and Flowers

There is not a season when edible plants cannot be found. Spring and summer is the prime seasons to forage for plants. Many varieties can be found, often in the same place. For the amateur forager, it's hard to imagine where to start looking, but the answer is simple – on your own doorstep. Even in gardens in town centres or on the sides of paths, there are many plants which are known to be weeds but in reality are edible wild foods.

When in the countryside, the best place to start looking is a hedgerow. Many hedgerows hold hundreds of species of plants and even animal life. A rough guide to the age of a hedgerow is that the amount of species found in a hedgerow equals its age.

Plants take on different forms through the seasons, and sometimes a picture or description in a guide may be different from what is seen. Here it is best to visit the same plant through the year to see the different forms it takes for yourself. It is then possible to make clear any positive identification. Many foragers will keep a calendar of plants found at different times of year. This is a good way to prepare for your trips out, to make a clear decision of what the you are aiming to find on a trip and where to start looking.

Of course different plants may taste good or bad to different people, but to further one's knowledge and opinions, I urge all readers of this guide to try as many species as they can, and understand what benefits can found in eating wild foods; it's not only shops that provide fresh greens for the table!

# Dandelion ☺

*Taraxacum officinale*
*5 – 40 cm | All year*

This perennial plant is known to most as a weed, but its potential is greatly underestimated. It grows almost anywhere, from pastures to meadows, waysides, roadsides, and garden lawns. The yellow flowers are indistinguishable, which in some places have two periods of flowering, which seed in later stages of its life, also known to children as "fairies". The young leaves seem to have a never-ending supply of growth, which can be found most of the year.

## What To Do

- The flowers make an excellent wine.
- The best part of the flowers is the middle, which when picked on a sunny day, make fantastic eating.
- The young leaves are excellent in salads.
- The young leaves dried out make a great herbal tea.
- The roots can be roasted until brittle and then ground up as a coffee substitute.

18

# Nettle ☺

*Urticaceae*
*Up to 1.5 m | Feb – October*

Nettle is a perennial which has many uses. The nettle is renowned to have stinging hairs on it which can irritate the skin. It is found in a vast range of nutrient soils, as well as roadsides, fields, allotments, gardens, and waysides. It Flowers from July to October.

## What To Do

- The young leaves from February, dried out, make a fantastic morning herbal tea.
- The young shoots make a famous beer, which can be drunk within a day but is best after a week. About 30 handfuls boiled in a gallon of water, sieved with 50 g of cream of tartar added, a kilo of sugar, and half an ounce of yeast, will sort it out. Then let nature do the rest.
- The young leaves make a fantastic soup.
- The seeds are very good in soups and stews.
- The seeds are good dried out and made into a tea.

# ☺ **Great Reed Mace / Cat's Tail**

*Typha latifolica*
*up to 3 m | All year*

This large sedge is usually found in ponds and slow-moving water that contains, mud, silt, or soil. At all times of the year, there is a use for this plant. Its name Cat's tail, derives from its seed head, which resembles a cats tail.

## What To Do

- The young, green seed head can be cooked like corn on the cob.
- The young stem contains a tasty inner core.
- Some plants hold a white grub, which is edible.
- The rhizome root system is high in carbohydrates and tastes very good after being roasted on a fire.

19

# ☺ **Soft Rush / Bulrush**

*Scirpus lacustris*
*up to 1 m | All year*

A hardy rush which is found at all times of the year and flowers from May to September. It is found where the ground is constantly damp – from ponds to damp meadows, river banks, roadside brooks, fields, and gardens.

## What To Do

- The only part of this plant to eat is the roots. Although they can be tough to dig up, they are worth while eating after putting them on a fire until cooked.

# Wood Sorrel ☺

*Oxalis acetosella*
*up to 10 cm | March – September*

A perennial that grows in some dark places and favours very damp conditions. Found widespread in forests, woodlands, and sometimes in tree line fields. Although edible, this plant must be eaten in moderation because it contains oxalic acid (from where its name derives from), which can cause upset stomach and, in worse cases, kidney stones. Flowers from April to May.

## What To Do

- The flowers taste best, giving a perfect line of sourness. Good on salads.
- The leaves can be picked in moderation and added to salads, or made into a soup.
- The leaves and flowers can be used to garnish.

20

# Japanese Rose-hip / Ramanas Rose ☺

*Rosa Rugosa*
*Up to 4 m | June – September*

Belonging to the rose family, it is known in some places of Europe and America as a beach or sea tomato. Although a native to China, Japan, and Korea, it is well worth including this plant because its vitamin and antioxidant level are extremely high, which is a great benefit. Although mainly found as part of ornamental gardens, some examples have found themselves growing in the wild, sometimes near parks and even as part of hedgerows. They are instantly recognisable by their large, reddish pinkish fruits. Like with the English rosehip, it is best to avoid eating the seeds due to their fine irritating hairs. It flowers from May to July.

## What To Do

- The rose petals can be made into a wine or syrup.
- The fruits can be made in a wine or eaten straight from the plant,
- The fruits can be made into syrup. Pick a few handfuls, mix with 6 ounces of sugar, and 1.5 cups of water, and boil on a gentle heat for 10 minutes. Strain and allow to cool.

# ☺ **Chickweed Family**

*Caryophyllaceae*
*up to 80 cm | February – November*

An annual growing plant. There are a number of species of chickweed, but all are recognisable as the chickweed family by their flowering petals, which consists of five sepals joined together in a tube. All are excellent eating, resembling lettuce in taste. It can be found in a variety of conditions but seems to favour damp fields, pastures, and meadows. It sometimes likes fertilised ground, such as a farmland.

## What To Do

- They can be added to sandwiches and salads.
- They can be used as a "green manure" for gardens and allotments. Digging them into the ground will fertilise your soil for growing plants, as well as produce further crops of chickweed.
- They are best eaten raw, straight after picking.

21

# ☺ **Watercress**

*Rorippa nasturtium-aquaticum*
*20 to 80 cm | May – October*

An herbaceous perennial, watercress is a fine wild food to be picked. It has many culinary uses, either cooked or uncooked. When found, the plants are usually found growing in large mats, and a large quantity can be picked at once. With a peppery taste, watercress is very much worth the picking. It is found throughout Staffordshire. As the name suggests, it is found growing around water sources with slow-flowing water, such as canals, feeders, lakes, reservoirs, rivers, streams, and brook edges.

## What To Do

- The plant can be used to make a soup.
- The plant can be eaten raw.
- The plant can be added to salads.
- It can be used to make sauces and pestos.

# Wild Garlic / Ramson ☺

*Allium satiuum*
*10 to 30 cm| May – July*

A perennial that is not hard to miss. The pungent smell of this plant fills the air of riverside woodlands and damp, broad-leafed woodlands. All parts of this plant are edible and usually grow in huge mats. The medicinal properties are unmatched and also have many culinary uses. Rubbing the leaves or flowers between the hands will release the strong smelling flavours, if you cannot already smell it. Wild garlic is a member of the lily family, and its two lookalikes – Lily of the Valley and Meadow Saffron – should not be confused with it, because it could result in fatality. If you are ever in doubt, do not pick this plant.

## What To Do

- The flowers are fantastic added to salads.
- The leaves are good in salads.
- The leaves can be chopped and added to sour cream and used as a dipping sauce.
- The flowers can be dried out and used in soups, stews, etc.
- The bulbs can be added to culinary dishes the same as normal garlic bought from shops.
- All parts of the plant can be eaten raw.

22

# Jack-by-the-Hedge / Hedge Garlic / Garlic Mustard ☺

*Alliaria petio lata*
*20 cm –1m |April – July*

This plant is an annual that is very similar in taste to wild garlic, although it has no relation. The taste is just the right power of "garlicness" and therefore can be used in a number of ways. This plant favours country lanes, where it can be found in large numbers. It is a common plant to find amongst hedgerows, but it can also be found in shady places, on woodland edges, gardens, and town and country parks, where the soil is nitrogen rich.

## What To Do

- The leaves can be eaten raw.
- The leaves can be chopped finely and added to salads or as garnish.
- The flowers are good tasting and can be eaten and used similarly to the leaves.
- The seeds, when matured, are black in colour and can be crushed in a pestle and mortar and used as pepper.

# ☺ **Grasses and Sedges**

*up to 1.5 m | March – November*

The most abundant source of plants in this guide, growing in virtually every location within Staffordshire. From gardens, to towns, parks, moors, fields, ponds, and cities, grasses and sedges are a perfect example of how nature can be just as opportunistic as we are. We cultivate some species for our own use and to feed animals which we eat, but many species have little to offer. However, their success to grow in almost every habitat means that we will never be in short supply.

## What To Do

- The young shoots of many species cab be picked and eaten as a snack.
- Many species contain seeds, which can be harvested in great numbers and ground into flour.
- Many species contain oats, which can be ground down to one's liking for porridge.

23

# ☺ **Rosebay Willowherb**

*Epilobium angustifolium*
*Up to 1.8 m | June – September*

A perennial which occupies a large range of habitats, from riverbank sides to waste grounds, country lanes and parks. This plant is very often seen growing in large numbers. This is thanks to its hairy seeds, which can fly up to seven miles from its mother plant. The rosebay willowherb is a plant that is instantly recognisable and has very little chance of confusion with other species.

## What To Do

- The young flowers can be made into a tea.
- The young flowers can be eaten raw or added to salads.
- The young shoots can steamed like asparagus.

# Clover ☺

*Pratense*
*5 to 20 cm | April – September*

A perennial that is very successful. White and red clover are very abundant in nutrient rich soils and can be found in a variety of habitats. The clover leaf is seen as great importance in Ireland, and it is also the national symbol. It can be found in meadows, wastelands, parks, gardens, and arable fields.

## What To Do

- The leaves are good eating as part of salads.
- The flower heads are good as part of salads or garnish.
- A wine can be made from the flower heads.

24

# Shepherd's Purse ☺

*Capsella bursa-pastoris*
*10 – 40 cm | March – December*

An annual or biennial that is quite successful in places which many plants may find it too hard to grow. Its heart-shaped leaves make it instantly recognisable, and its peppery taste is easy to overcome. It grows in rocky places, fields, pastures, gardens with little soil, meadows, and towns and cities.

## What To Do

- The leaves and flowers are good in salads.
- The whole plant can be cooked as a vegetable and added to courses.
- Both the leaves and flowers are good in stews as flavouring.

# ☺ **Horseradish / Red Cole**

*Armoracia rusticana*
*5 – 40 cm | September – November*

A perennial that has a fantastic taste. It originates from south-eastern Europe but has been introduced to the UK and soon spread. It is now found on roadsides, paths, scrubland, wasteland, river banks, and roadside brooks. It is one of the few plants to be aware of in this guide, due to its similar looks to the dock leaf. The horseradish is distinguished by its fresh, waxy-looking leaves as opposed to the dock leaf, which has red tints throughout it and very often red stems. (See the Ten No-Nos on page 76 for more details on dock leaves.)

## What To Do

- The roots can be harvested in September and made into horseradish sauce. Finely grate the roots and then add seasoning, crème fraiche, a tablespoon of vinegar, a tablespoon of English mustard, and a pinch of sugar. Mix all together and leave to infuse for 20 minutes, then serve immediately.
- The young leaves in early summer can be eaten in salads.

25

# ☺ **Lamb's Cress / Wood or Hairy Bitter Cress**

*Cardamine flexuosa*
*Up to 15 cm | All Year*

Also known to be a herb, this plant is advantageous to one looking for wild foods in winter, as it stays green all year. The best time for picking is January to March. Because it is a member of the mustard family, the leaves are not to everyone's liking. They are found in damp and shady places and quite often are found in disturbed ground; often they appear in gardens as a "weed".

## What To Do

- The leaves can be eaten raw.
- The leaves can be cooked like spinach, but using saltwater if the bitterness needs to be lessened.
- The flowers are best and can be eaten raw.
- The flowers can be added to salads or as garnish.

# Himalayan Balsam / Indian Balsam ☺

*Impatiens glandulifera*
*up to 2.5 m | June – August*

A perennial that is a prime example of how an invasive species can soon come to decimate native species. This plant originated in Asia, but since being introduced to Britain, it has congregated and in some cases completely taken over river banks, wetlands, and damp and moist places near water sources. However, it is worth noting that this plant has edible uses, although not to everyone's liking. The stems have been rumoured to be slightly toxic, although older species should never be picked in any cases.

## What To Do

- The young stems can be cooked like asparagus, but with a change of water.
- The seeds and young flowers can be eaten raw.
- The flowers can be used to make a wine.

# Violets ☺

*Violaceae*
*5 to 10 cm | All Year*

A perennial, the violet is yet another gift for Staffordshire, being available all year. Flowering between March and June, the violet is found in damp, shady places where the soil is nutrient rich, often in or on the edges of woodland (apart from the hairy violet, which favours dry grasslands). Violets are heavily involved with the perfume industry, and they also do have edible benefits and are worth the search.

## What To Do

- The young leaves can be eaten raw, or they can be cooked like spinach.
- The flowers can be eaten raw.
- The flowers can be crystallised. To do this, whisk an egg white with a couple drops of rose water. Coat the violets in the mixture and cover with sugar. Leave to dry overnight, and your treat is ready.

## ☺ **Lavender**

*Lavandula angustifolia*
*20 to 60 cm | May – September*

A shrub, the lavender is a fantastic plant that has many medicinal and culinary uses. Its essential oil extracts have been, and still are, a major part of the perfume and cleaning product industry. Lavender is a major production plant in France, but the English version (although not native to England) is grown in gardens and outside of city and town buildings, as part of an ornamental garden.

### What To Do

- The leaves can be used to make a herbal tea.
- The leaves can be dried out and used as part of a 'herbs de Provence' bouquet for cooking with various recipes for flavouring.
- A fantastic dessert called lavender crème brûlée can be made.

## ☺ **Chives, Onions, and Leeks**

*Allium*
*Up to 1.2 m | May – September*

An herbaceous perennial, the allium family is a true wonder food of Staffordshire. Its uses are almost endless, and they are one of the most commonly used food sources by the majority of Staffordshire people. Although finding rogue onions and leeks that have continued to grow on old, nutrient-rich allotment sites and gardens can be tricky, its cousin the chive can be found growing wild in damp rocky places, on sandy areas, and riverbanks and roadside brooks.

### What To Do

Below are a list of the few favourite ways to eat the allium, but in reality the list is endless.

- Onion soup is a classic favourite that is easily made.
- Onions can be added to quiches.
- A pie can be made from Leek and potato.
- Leeks are fantastic prepared the same as or with cauliflower cheese.
- Chives are fantastic added as part of salads.
- Onions are good, thrown straight onto a fire until blackened all over.
- Onions and leeks are excellent chopped up finely and added to salads.
- Onions are very good made part of curries and Chinese meals.
- Onions are excellent as part of the mince beef and onion pie recipe.
- The flowers from the chive and onion can be added to salads.
- Caramelised onion can be made from reducing down onion, with sugar and vinegar.
- Onions are a favourite as part of chutneys.
- All parts of leeks, onions and chives are edible.

# Thyme ☺

*Thymus*
*5 – 40 cm | April – October*

A perennial, the thymus family is a great success of Staffordshire, found in a variety of habitats. The thyme has long been used in the culinary industry and is very much worth picking. It is found on damp meadows, old and disused quarries, pastures, gardens, meadows and embankments, and on the side of town, city, and village roads, often in large groups.

## What To Do

- It can be dried and used as a kitchen herb.
- The leaves and flowers can be added to salads.
- It can be added to stews and pies as flavouring.
- It can be sprinkled onto chips and roast potatoes before cooking in the oven for excellent results.

28

# Mint ☺

*Mentha*
*Up to 90 cm | June – September*

An herbaceous perennial, the mint is a fantastic wild food source that has many culinary uses. Found throughout Staffordshire, it is a plant that is worth picking for its smells as well as its taste. There are many species of the mint family, and some have a more distinct smell than others – for example the peppermint, which is grown as a garden herb, is the most prized of the mint family. The wild cousins are also worth picking and are found in abundance, where the nutrient-rich soils allow. Mints can be found in gardens, country parks, towns and cities, woodlands, near rivers and water, hedgerows, waysides, and limestone soils.

## What To Do

- The leaves and flowers can be added to boiling water to make a fantastic herbal tea.
- The leaves can be chopped with other herbs to make part of a marinade rub for joints of meat, before roasting in the oven.
- Mint sauce can be made by finely chopping a couple handfuls of leaves, mixing with vinegar and a teaspoon of sugar, and leaving for 10 minutes. Serve immediately with lamb or on a sandwich.

# ☺ **Lemon Balm**

*Melissa officinalis*
*up to 90 cm | June – October*

An herbaceous perennial, lemon balm is another member of the mint family, and it highly resembles it. Although not a native to the UK, it has spread with great success and is a popular herb to be grown in gardens and allotment. The plant has a distinct lemon smell to it but not overpowering, and it can be used in similar ways to mint.

## What To Do

- The leaves and stalks can be dried and used to make a herbal tea.
- The leaves can be finely chopped and added and joints of meat before roasting.
- The leaves can be used with mint to give a lemony twist to mint sauce.
- The leaves can be added to pizzas for a Mediterranean twist.

29

# ☺ **Dog Rose / Rosehip**

*Rosa cania*
*Up to 4 m | May – July*

This shrub grows successfully in hedgerows and is very often part of garden plants. As well of having fruits that are of high importance, the flowers can also be used in a variety of ways that make this plant worth the pick.

## What To Do

- The flowers can be made into syrup.
- The flowers can be made into rose water.
- The flowers can be made into a wine.
- The flowers can be eaten raw.
- The flowers can be eaten or added as part of salads.

# Marigolds ☺

*Calendula officinalis*
*up to 90 cm | June – October*

An annual, the marigold is grown by many Staffordshire folk as a wildflower feature, garden borders, or in pots inside and out. Escapees from gardens can also be found in country parks and on waste grounds. The flowers are the only part that can be eaten and have a distinctive lemony flavour.

## What To Do

- The flowers can be eaten raw.
- The flowers can be added to salads or as garnish.
- The flowers, dried or fresh, can be added to ice cubes and added to drinks as a refreshing drink.
- The flowers can be made into syrup.
- The flowers can be made into a wine.
- The flowers have been used to flavour butter. To do this, take a couple handfuls of petals and add half its weight in softened butter, leave to infuse for a couple weeks, then use.

30

# Heathers ☺

*Calluna / Erica*
*50 cm – 1 m | June – October*

A perennial shrub, this plant is an excellent addition to the Staffordshire larder. Although not unique, it does hold a valuable place within the food chain, particularly for bees for its pollen and nectar. At the height of the flowering season, the Staffordshire Moorlands is quite a breathtaking sight of a purple sea, which is captured on many visiting cameras. The heather has been used for thousands of years by man and is very much worth using as a seasonal treat. The flowers are the part that is used, but they can taste slightly dry and require a certain palette. Heathers can be found on acidy soils, mainly on moorlands but also on heaths, cliff edges, grasslands, and occasionally in pine forests.

## What To Do

- When the flowers are at their most open, the pollen can be collected in great quantities by shaking into a bag. Use it to make dampers.
- The flowers can be picked, dried, and made into a herbal tea.
- An old recipe, called heather ale, can be made from the flowers.

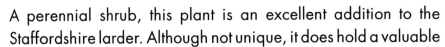

## ☺ **Poppy**

*Papaver rhoeas*
*up to 70 cm | May – July*

An annual, the poppy is a delightful flower, and its arrival usually heralds that summer is beginning. Various types of poppy can be found and are edible. The flowers and seed heads are the parts that are used. Poppies can be found in meadows, wastelands, gardens, country lanes, and corn fields.

### What To Do

- The flowers can be made into a tea.
- The petals can be made into syrup.
- The seeds can be used to make poppy seed cake.
- The seeds can be added to breads.

31

## ☺ **Evening Primrose/ Fever Plant / King's-Cure-All/ Night Willow-herb / Scabish / Scurvish**

*Oenothera biennis*
*Up to 5 ft | June – September*

A biennial, the primrose is a plant that is favoured by gardeners. The whole of the plant is edible, which makes it very much worth picking. The plant can also be found wild, usually in scrublands and railway embankments, but it also can be found in urban environments, wastelands, and old abandoned car parks and quarries that are overgrown.

### What To Do

- Primrose oil can be extracted from the plant and used in cooking.
- The flowers can be used to make a tea.
- The petals can be eaten in salads.
- The young buds can be used in salads.
- The buds and flowers can be dried and used as a herbal tea.
- The roots can be chopped and used in salads.
- The seeds can be roasted and ground down and used as flour or as a topping on breads or salads.

# Daisy ☺

*Bellin perennis*
*5 – 15 cm | April – September*

A perennial, it is not surprising that the daisy is also used as a wild food through its great abundance. It has been used for centuries, and despite its small size and little use these days, it is one of the most highly recognised flowers to be found. It is found almost everywhere in Staffordshire, from country lanes to fields, gardens, wastelands, cultivated lands, golf courses, meadows, and between cracks of pavements in towns and cities.

## What To Do

- The flowers can be used in salads.
- The young leaves can be used in salads.
- The flower petals can be dried and used as a herbal tea.
- A wine can be made from the flowers.

32

# Vetches ☺

*Vicia*
*50 cm – 1.5 m | April – October*

A perennial, vetches are a common wildflower in late spring and through the summer months in Staffordshire. A member of the pea family, the flowers, leaves, and seed pods are used. It should be noted that if using the seeds, only the young, tender green specimens should be collected, as the seeds develop toxins as they mature. Always cook the seeds before consuming. They are found in meadows, country lanes, woodland and roadside verges, wastelands, and riverbanks.

## What To Do

- The flowers can be eaten raw.
- The flowers can be added to salads.
- The leaves and tendrils can be eaten raw.
- The seeds can be boiled and used like peas.

*Pete Bridgwood*

## ☺ Cleavers / Goosegrass

*Gallium aparine*
*up to 1 m| March – May*

An annual, this plant is very well-known amongst youngsters as sticking mercilessly to clothing. Usually found amongst nettles, the cleaver thrives in nitrogen-rich soils. It is useful to know that this plant is often found growing in a tangled mess, as its thin stem cannot support its weight and thus becomes knotted together. Cleavers can be found on roadside verges, meadows, wastelands, allotments, river and brook banks, hedgerows, and uncultivated abandoned lands.

### What To Do

- The young stems and leaves can be boiled to destroy the hook-like hairs and used as a vegetable.
- The seeds can be roasted, ground down, and used as a coffee substitute.

33

## ☺ Garden Roses

*Rosa spp*
*Up to 2 m | April – August*

A shrub, garden roses are as popular and common with gardeners as the pansy, and they add a fantastic, colourful addition to garden borders or as part of a floral display. Although they have quite sharp thorns, they are also great eating and can be used throughout their flowering season. They are found through Staffordshire and are easily recognised.

### What To Do

- The young flowers can be eaten raw.
- The flowers can be added to salads.
- The flowers can be made into a syrup.
- The flowers can be made into rose water.
- The flowers can be used to infuse cooking oil.
- The wildflowers can be used to make a wine.

# Ground Elder / Goutweed ☺

*Aegopodium podagraria*
*50 cm – 1 m | All year*

A perennial, this plant has no relation to the elder tree/bush, despite looking the same and having a similar name. Ground elder was originally grown as a pot herb, but it soon spread and now is a common site throughout the countryside. Its taste is not to everyone's liking but soon can be palatable. It is found mainly in hedgerows and roadside verges throughout Staffordshire.

## What To Do

- The leaves can be cooked with butter and used as a vegetable.
- The leaves can be cooked like spinach and used as a vegetable.

# Thistles ☺

*Cirsium Spp*
*Up to 1.5 m | June – October*

An annual to biennial, thistles are a common site throughout Staffordshire. To many it is known to be a thorny, useless weed, but in fact thistles played a large history to our ancestors as a food source. Although it is covered in spines, they are easily taken off by using a knife. All of the plant can be used, with the exception of the marsh thistle, whose roots are not edible. Thistles can be commonly found in meadows, waste grounds, country lanes, arable lands, hedgerows, and in large gardens, all where the nutrient-rich soils allow.

## What To Do

- The flowers can be eaten raw.
- The flowers can be added to salads.
- The stems can be eaten raw.
- The stems can be cooked like asparagus.
- The flowers can be made into a herbal tea.
- The stems can be made into a herbal tea.
- The roots can be roasted as a source of carbohydrate.

# ☺ **Burdock / Greater Burdock**

*Actium Spp*
*up to 1.5 m | September – December*

A widely common biennial, this plant is yet another fine example of an important wild food source to be found in Staffordshire. The roots are the parts to be used of this plant, which can grow to considerable sizes. The second year growth is the best time to harvest the roots. Its flowers resemble that of thistles, but its leaves do not, being quite large. The flower heads are also quite sticky and often cling to unaware passers-by and animals, which help distribute its seeds. The spines of the flower heads were the inspiration for the development of Velcro in the 1950s. The burdock can be found on country paths, scrub lands, wastelands, hedgerows, country lane verges, woodland verges, riverbanks, and limestone dales, usually where man has set foot.

### What To Do

- The roots can be eaten raw.
- The roots can be cooked on a fire and eaten like potato.
- The roots can be added to soups and stews.
- The roots can be stored like potatoes throughout the winter.

35

# ☺ **Plantains**

*Plantago major spp*
*20 – 30 cm | February – October*

A perennial, the plantain family is a well-established meadow plant, where its seeds are easily spread. Plantains do not have a well-documented history, but they certainly do have great food potential, which no doubt was used by our ancestors. All members of the plantain family are edible and can be found in great abundance, which makes it very much worth picking. Plantains can be found in meadows, wastelands, grasslands, paths, roadsides, in towns and cities, gardens, and riverbanks.

### What To Do

- The leaves can be made into a herbal tea.
- The leaves can be dried for tea, which can be stored for many months.
- The seeds can be ground down to make flour.

# Blackberry / Bramble ☺

*Rubus fruticosus*
*up to 2 m | March – July*

A shrub that is as familiar as a weed as it is a successful fruiting plant, the bramble is widely known for its thorny stems and of course its high-yielding fruits. The stems are not as commonly used but are very much worth picking because they are not in short supply and make excellent eating. Brambles are widespread and can be found in overgrown gardens, hedgerows, meadows, country lanes, towns and cities, riversides, and country parks.

## What To Do

- The young stems can be cooked like asparagus.
- The young leaves can be dried and made into a herbal tea.

36

# Raspberry ☺

*Rubus idaeus*
*Up to 2 m | February – October*

A shrub, the raspberry leaves have a long history of been used for many bodily problems. They are very common and appear to take a step back during colder months, until the heat of the sun throws them back into growth during warm months, where they appear to be everywhere. When picking the leaves, they do look remarkably like bramble leaves; however, they do not contain large thorns and grow upright on single canes. They are found in country parks, meadow borders, wastelands, path verges, large gardens, woodland verges – all where the nutrient-rich soil allows.

## What To Do

- The leaves dry quite well and can be saved over winter months.
- The leaves are traditionally used to make a herbal tea. Infuse either the dry or fresh leaves in boiling water for 5 minutes, then drink. It can be sweetened with a little honey.

# ☺ **Meadowsweet**

*Filipendula ulmaria*
*50 cm – 1.5 m | April – October*

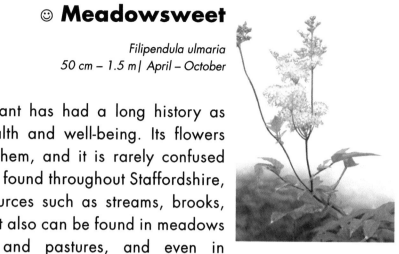

An herbaceous perennial, this plant has had a long history as being an important herb for health and well-being. Its flowers have a pleasant honey smell to them, and it is rarely confused with other plants. Quite commonly found throughout Staffordshire, it is mainly found near water sources such as streams, brooks, rivers, wetlands, and ditches, but it also can be found in meadows and pastures, and even in wildflower allotments and country parks.

## What To Do

- The leaves can be dried out and stored for use over the winter.
- The leaves and flowers can be used to make a herbal tea.

38

# Trees

There was once a time not so long ago when trees dominated our landscape. Virtually the whole of the country was part of the same forest. Deciduous trees made most of this great forest; oak, beech, and silver birch are just a couple of the most impressive types. As man evolved, we coppiced and eventually felled many parts of the great forest, clearing them for cultivating land, sometimes only leaving single trees such as oaks to grow to great giants, many up to a thousand years old.

Now a shadow of its former self, trees still make up an iconic part of our countryside, their leaves soaking up carbon dioxide and converting it into oxygen. However, in many cases they are cut down for timber.

Amongst their many uses, trees also have the benefit of yielding fruits, nuts, and sap, which we can use for our consumption. Nature also takes advantage of this, so careful consideration must be made before harvesting many fruits, nuts, or sap from the same species.

However, it is certain that trees are of great important to man, so it is worth every effort to harvest the goods that trees can provide for us.

# Hawthorn ☺

*Cratageus laevigata*
*up to 10 m | March – May*

The hawthorn is one of the most successful trees used in Staffordshire. Due to the high number of hedgerows, the hawthorn is the tree that is used to make most of these hedgerows up. From around March, the buds of the hawthorn begin to sprout, heralding the call of spring and the explosion of life within the natural world. Hawthorn can be found all over Staffordshire, as hedgerows in the countryside to wild trees growing in meadows and fields. It is regularly used as an ornamental tree in gardens.

## What To Do

Apart from the berries, the other parts of the hawthorn used are the leaves and the flowers.

- The young buds are best and can be added to salads.
- The young leaves can be added to salads or eaten as a passing snack.
- The flowers can be eaten raw.
- The flowers can be added to salads.
- The flowers can be made into a wine.

40

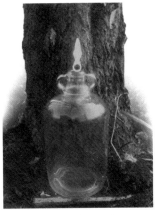

# Silver Birch ☺

*Belula pendula*
*8 – 25 m | March*

A native tree the silver birch is one of the most important trees. It has almost limitless uses within the bushcraft scene and is very important to wildlife. The silver birch has been used by man for generations; it also can be used as a food source. They are found everywhere in Staffordshire – villages, towns, cities, country parks, hedgerows, woodland, forests, moors, and wastelands.

## What To Do

- The catkins can be eaten raw.
- The young leaves can be made into an herbal tea.
- During the spring, when the sap is rising, it can be tapped and drunk straight, or made into a classic wine. Always remember to plug any holes made in the tree, to avoid it bleeding to death.

## ☺ **Sycamore**

*Acar pseudoplatanus*
*25 – 30 m | March*

This native deciduous tree is of high importance within the furniture industry. It also plays a major part of importance for wildlife, especially within deciduous woodland. Sycamores can be found in woodlands, country lane borders, country parks, and sometimes in towns and cities as an ornamental tree or border tree.

### What To Do

- The sap can be tapped in the same way as silver birch. To tap a tree for it sap, there are two methods   drill a small hole in about 9 inches off the ground and about 1 inch deep, or make a few small slashes with a knife in a vertical row about 2 cm apart. The sap should instantly start to run. To collect, place a container underneath. To channel the sap, the best way to do this is to carve or used an improvised funnel.

  A couple rules to remember when tapping trees for sap. Only tap either silver birch or sycamore, always fill any holes made, and only use mature trees and not saplings.

  If the sap does not run, it is either too late or too early. For best results, tap when the buds are appearing.

## ☺ **Elderflower**

*Sambucus nigra*
*Up to 10 m | June – August*

The elder is a seasonal shrub or small tree. When its flowers emerge, it heralds summer has arrived; when its fruits ripen, it heralds autumn has arrived. In folklore, the elder has been used for medicinal purposes for generations. Its flowers are also edible; they contain natural yeast and so would have been used to make home brews, when yeast was in short supply. The elder can be found in a variety of locations, from gardens to woodland verges, moors, garden features, towns, villages, and cities.

### What To Do

- The sap can be tapped in the same way as silver birch. To tap a tree for it sap, there are two methods   drill a small hole in about 9 inches off the ground and about 1 inch deep, or make a few small slashes with a knife in a vertical row about 2 cm apart. The sap should instantly start to run. To collect, place a container underneath. To channel the sap, the best way to do this is to carve or used an improvised funnel.

  A couple rules to remember when tapping trees for sap. Only tap either silver birch or sycamore, always fill any holes made, and only use mature trees and not saplings.

  If the sap does not run, it is either too late or too early. For best results, tap when the buds are appearing.

# Beech ☺

*Fagus sylvatica*
*25 – 30 m | April – May*

A native tree to Britain, the beech is one of the most important trees we have. As a hardwood tree, it has many uses within the furniture industry and also can prove useful for food when it starts to leaf. The beech can be found everywhere in Staffordshire – country parks, woodlands, and forests. Small species are used as parts of hedgerows or ornamental garden trees in villages, towns, and cities they are used as border trees or found down country lanes.

## What To Do

- The young leaves can be eaten raw for a snack.
- The young leaves can be added to salads.
- The young leaves can be used to make a classic alcoholic beverage called beech leaf noyau. To make it; fill a bottle three-quarters with the leaves and then fill with gin. Leave for 2 weeks and then strain. It has a banana liquor taste and is highly recommended.

42

# Lime / Linden ☺

*Tilia Spp*
*10 – 30 m | June – July*

The lime has been used for generations and is famed for its tea, to the point it has its own style of teapot. The leaves can sometimes be confused with other species of tree; however, the flowers are the only part to be used, and they cannot be confused with others. It is said that when the lime flowers, it is the sign of midsummer approaching. Limes are an important food source for insects, especially bees, which can be heard buzzing in the trees during flowering season. The lime can be found throughout Staffordshire, mainly in parks as ornamental trees, but they can be found on the fringes of woodlands, country parks, and sometimes large gardens.

## What To Do

- To make lime or linden tea, collect a handful of flowers in full bloom and place in a teapot of boiling water for 10 minutes, then serve immediately. For a better taste, add a teaspoon of honey.
- The leaves can be dried and used to make tea over non-flowering months.

# ☺ **Pine**

*Pinus spp*
*3 – 50 m | September – November*

A highly successful tree within Britain and quite possibly the largest, this tree has the largest concentration of sub-species within the family and is the most used for the furniture industry. The trees can be grown very close together for the production of wood, and when walking through such a man-made forest, they can turn daylight into night. The pine family has been a much sought after tree for centuries for its many medicinal and culinary uses and is very much worth using. Pines can be found everywhere in Staffordshire, from parks to gardens, woodlands, forests, cities, towns, and villages.

## What To Do

- The resin can be used as a chewing gum. But due to its stickiness, its best to have a little at the roof of the mouth and use the tongue to gets its taste.
- Pine needles can be used to make a pine tea.
- The rootlets have been eaten as an emergency food.
- Spruce beer can be made from spruce twigs. Mix around 50 spruce twigs with 400 g of sugar, 100 g of treacle, and a gallon of boiling water. Boil the twigs first in the water for half an hour and then add the other ingredients and a sprinkle of yeast when the liquid has cooled. Ferment in a bucket for a week, siphon into bottles, and leave for another week. Serve chilled.

43

# Fruits and Berries

Fruits are by far foragers' favourite food. Seasonal they made be, different species will appear at different times, combined, they are available at nearly all times of the year.

Most fruits appear in the summer, when the sun is hot and ripens the fruits to great sweetness. Here the forager has to bear in mind that they will not be the only ones competing to find a passing treat, as nature will also be taking advantage of this seasonal hoard of treats.

Most fruits will have a short fruiting season. On one trip out, some fruits will look to be just ripening – and on another day, they will all be gone, dropped to the ground and rotting or taken by nature. This is where foragers have to make their timing right. Of course, be mindful that taking all the apples on a tree will leave nature or others with nothing, so please don't take them all at once.

Many fruits, like the blackberry, are high in numbers, and there will be plenty for all, but they will start to rot after a couple days, even after being in the fridge, so careful and planned picking must be made.

The good thing with fruits is that they have many uses for sweets, jams, puddings, and more, and with a high number of species offering at once, inventive cooking is very possible.

For the amateur forager, fruits and berries can be associated with being poisons, but using this guide will make comparisons easy, and I do urge the reader to give the berry a chance and discover a new fruity favourite.

# Cherry ☺

*Prunus avium*
*up to 10 m | June – August*

The cherry is a well-known fruit, more a seasonal treat for many, but unknown to most, wild cherries and ornamental cherries grow wild in a variety of places. They are instantly recognisable by the bark or the leaves, and the fruits themselves are sweet and highly tasty. They are found in woodland fringes, towns, cities, and parks as border trees or ornamental garden trees.

## What To Do

Jams – Yes
Wines & Spirits – Yes
Dried Out – Yes
Herbal Teas – Yes
Pies & Crumbles – Yes
Eaten Raw – Yes
Sauces – Yes
Syrups & Cordials – Yes

# Hawthorn ☺

*Crataegus laevigata*
*Up to 10 m | September – March*

Hawthorn berries have long been associated with being poisonous. This is not the case. Hawthorn berries are an excellent wild food, and an important food source for birds. They are one of the few berries that can be found over the winter, and when ripened just right, they have an excellent taste and texture. They can be picked in great quantities and keep well. One excellent way to use them is to pick a generous quantity and squeeze the juice from them onto a baking tray, then either dry in a low oven or in the sun. They taste excellent, similar to sweets. They are a very common in hedgerows, grow as wild single trees, and can be found in meadows and steep bank sides throughout Staffordshire.

## What To Do

Jams – Yes
Wines & Spirits – Yes
Dried Out – Yes
Herbal Teas – Yes
Pies & Crumbles – No
Eaten Raw – Yes
Sauces – Yes
Syrups & Cordials – Yes

# ☺ **Elderberry**

*Sambucus nigra*
*Up to 10 m | August – October*

The Elderberry fruit, like all soft fruits, seems to have a quick fruiting season. They appear at the end of the summer in huge quantities, hanging from the trees, and they all seem to come at once. Collecting is not a problem because the fruits hang at the bottom for picking, whilst the ones higher up are left for wildlife. Elderberries have long been used for medicinal uses, and their culinary potential has many uses, too. They are found all across Staffordshire in parks, woodland fringes, towns, villages, cities, and even on the moors.

## What To Do

Jams – Yes

Wines & Spirits – Yes

Dried Out – Yes

Herbal Teas – Yes

Pies & Crumbles – Yes

Eaten Raw – No

Sauces – Yes

Syrups & Cordials – Yes

47

# ☺ **Wild Strawberry**

*Fragaria vesca*
*10 – 30 cm | June – August*

Although small, the wild strawberry is amongst the tastiest. Its ripest fruits have a taste similar to bubblegum, and its uses are exactly the same as the cultivated version. The strawberry has a long history but seems to be passed by in modern days; instead, many go for the fruits which provide large quantities. However, it is very much worth the picking for culinary uses or as a snack. Strawberries are a woodland plant and can be found in woodland and woodland verges all across Staffordshire.

## What To Do

Jams – Yes

Wines & Spirits – Yes

Dried Out – Yes

Herbal Teas – Yes

Pies & Crumbles – Yes

Eaten Raw – Yes

Sauces – Yes

Syrups & Cordials – Yes

# Crowberry ☺

*Empetrum nigrum*
Up to 20 cm | August – September

The first of The Staffordshire Larder's Moorland plants. The crowberry is a tough one to spot. Its berries are small and blend in well with its surrounding, often underneath foliage. When picked during their mid-growing season, they are a delight and have many uses. When the fruits are older, they adopt a woody centre and sometimes require a little water being added to them. When used for cooking, they work particularly well for fruit salads. They are found on acidic soils, mainly on the Moorlands in the Peak District. Sometimes they can be found on peaty, acidic soils dotted around Staffordshire, often on common/access lands.

**What To Do**

Jams – No
Wines & Spirits – Yes
Dried Out – Yes
Herbal Teas – Yes
Pies & Crumbles – Yes
Eaten Raw – Yes
Sauces – Yes
Syrups & Cordials – Yes

48

# Cowberry / Bearberry ☺

*Arctostaphylos ura-urs*
5 –15 cm | August – October

Yet another Moorland classic, but even less used than the crowberry. The cowberry is often overlooked due to its colour associated with being poisonous. However, this is far from the truth. The cowberry makes excellent eating, particularly as a snack, and its uses are very similar to those of the bilberry. When not in flower or fruit, they can be hard to spot because the leaves are almost an exact replica of bilberries and often grow together to. The difference is that cowberry leaves are lighter and fresher in colour. The cowberry is mainly found on the Moorlands in the Peak District and in high-acidic soils dotted around Staffordshire.

**What To Do**

Jams – Yes
Wines & Spirits – Yes
Dried Out – Yes
Herbal Teas – Yes
Pies & Crumbles – Yes
Eaten Raw – Yes
Sauces – Yes
Syrups & Cordials – Yes

## ☺ **Bilberry**

*Vaccimium myrtillus*
*5 – 20 cm | July – September*

The bilberry is a classic summer fruit which is only found on acidic soils. Travelling to the Roaches Escarpment or its other nearby escarpments, Hen Cloud, or Ramshaw Rocks during hot summer days will guarantee one to witness a hoard of folk rummaging in the bushes and picking bilberries. Very popular within the Polish community, it has caught on fast with everyone else and is an excellent family activity. Bilberries mainly grow on the Moorlands found in the Peak District; however, where the conditions allow, they can be found on access lands dotted around Staffordshire and down many country lanes and woodland fringes.

### What To Do

Jams – Yes

Wines & Spirits – Yes

Dried Out – Yes

Herbal Teas – Yes

Pies & Crumbles – Yes

Eaten Raw – Yes

Sauces – Yes

Syrups & Cordials – Yes

49

## ☺ **Raspberry**

*Rubus ideaus*
*Up to 2 m | May – August*

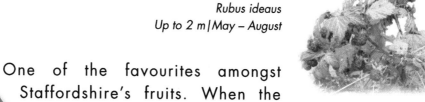

One of the favourites amongst Staffordshire's fruits. When the fruits first ripen, they seem to be around for many months, and then they disappear as quickly as they arrive. An absolute classic that can be found all across Staffordshire, mainly in hedgerows on country lanes, but also in parks, allotments, and gardens.

### What To Do

Jams – Yes

Wines & Spirits – Yes

Dried Out – Yes

Herbal Teas – Yes

Pies & Crumbles – Yes

Eaten Raw – Yes

Sauces – Yes

Syrups & Cordials – Yes

# Blackberry ☺

*Rubus fruilicosus*
*Up to 2 m | August – November*

The most recommended of *The Staffordshire Larder's* fruits, the blackberry is an extremely common fruit which is found from the summer onwards into the autumn. It is rich in history for medicinal uses, and its culinary potential has long been recognised. Blackberries are amongst the most recognisable fruits, and they are also known for being very invasive, quite often taking over large patches of rough scrublands, and their forbidding thorns create their own defence. Blackberries are found throughout Staffordshire – woodlands and forests, wastelands, hedgerows, field boundaries, gardens, town centres, cities and villages, and on river, brook, and stream borders.

### What To Do

Jams – Yes
Wines & Spirits – Yes
Dried Out – Yes
Herbal Teas – Yes
Pies & Crumbles – Yes
Eaten Raw – Yes
Sauces – Yes
Syrups & Cordials – Yes

50

# Sloe / Blackthorn ☺

*Prunus spinosa*
*Up to 5 m | August – October*

On first glance, sloes appear to be excellent eating, but upon trying, frowns often appear because the extremely bitter tannins dry the mouth out. Sloes need taming, and the best method for this is to cook with sugar. They are particularly ideal for syrups and liquors. A famous liquor known as sloe gin is easily made by infusing sloes with gin for at least three months. Sloes can be found on woodland margins and scrublands throughout Staffordshire, often as part of hedgerows.

### What To Do

Jams – Yes
Wines & Spirits – Yes
Dried Out – No
Herbal Teas – Yes
Pies & Crumbles – Yes
Eaten Raw – No
Sauces – Yes
Syrups & Cordials – Yes

## ☺ **Plum**

*Prunus*
*Up to 4 m | August – September*

Many different varieties of plum are grown in Staffordshire, and all are edible and are excellent eating. Their mellow and sometimes sweet taste are as much sought after by nature (particularly wasps), as well by as the people that grow them. Some species have strayed from the gardens into the hedgerows for walkers to enjoy. Plums are mainly found in gardens as an ornament plant, but also in allotments as orchids. Sometimes they can be found on country lanes, often close to the mother plants.

### What To Do

Jams – Yes

Wines & Spirits – Yes

Dried Out – No

Herbal Teas – Yes

Pies & Crumbles – Yes

Eaten Raw – No

Sauces – Yes

Syrups & Cordials – Yes

51

## ☺ **Rosehip / Dogrose**

*Rosa Spp*
*Up to 4 m | September – October*

During the Second World War, locals were given recipes for using rosehips to extract its high source of Vitamin C. It was and is a wonder food. Rosehips are one of the only surviving sources of food through the winter months. Vitally important to local wildlife, it also has many uses for the kitchen. Rosehips are best picked after the first frosts because a frost will mature (sweeten and soften) the fruiting bodies, making them excellent for eating on the move. They have a rich strawberry taste to them, but in reality the taste is unique. One word of caution is to remove the hairy seeds within, because they can cause severe irritation to the throat and can cause coughing fits. The best place to find them is in hedgerows, but they can also be found on woodland borders, as well as in towns, cities and villages as ornamental plants and down country lanes.

### What To Do

Jams – Yes

Wines & Spirits – Yes

Dried Out – Yes

Herbal Teas – Yes

Pies & Crumbles – Yes

Eaten Raw – Yes

Sauces – Yes

Syrups & Cordials – Yes

# Quince ☺

*Cydonia oblonga*
*Up to 8 m | September – November*

Native to south-western Asia, quince is mainly found as an ornamental garden tree, and it is worth noting that this fruit has in many places escaped from the gardens and gone wild. The quince is very much underrated; its taste is unlike no other, and its texture is similar to apple. It makes very good eating in chutneys and sauces. Although it can be eaten raw, caution should be made as to the quantity eaten, because too much can cause upset stomach. Quince trees often are small enough to be classified as a shrub, and they can easily be pruned to keep under control. They are found in many gardens all over Staffordshire, and when found in the wild, their flowers will automatically identify it. In the wild it can be found near woodland fringes, quite often near civilisation.

**What To Do**

Jams – No
Wines & Spirits – Yes
Dried Out – No
Herbal Teas – Yes
Pies & Crumbles – Yes
Eaten Raw – No
Sauces – Yes
Syrups & Cordials – Yes

52

# Damson / Bullace ☺

*Prunus domestica subspilnstitia*
*Up to 6 m | August – October*

Yet another Moorland classic, but even less used than the crowberry. The cowberry is often overlooked due to its colour associated with being poisonous. However, this is far from the truth. The cowberry makes excellent eating, particularly as a snack, and its uses are very similar to those of the bilberry. When not in flower or fruit, they can be hard to spot because the leaves are almost an exact replica of bilberries and often grow together to. The difference is that cowberry leaves are lighter and fresher in colour. The cowberry is mainly found on the Moorlands in the Peak District and in high-acidic soils dotted around Staffordshire.

**What To Do**

Jams – Yes
Wines & Spirits – Yes
Dried Out – Yes
Herbal Teas – Yes
Pies & Crumbles – Yes
Eaten Raw – Yes
Sauces – Yes
Syrups & Cordials – Yes

## ☺ **Green Gage / Bullace**

*Prunus domestica*
*Up to 4 m | August – September*

Greengages are amongst the best tasting of the Prunus family. Very similar to the growing situations of damsons, their colour resembles their name: they are green at first but turn slightly yellowish with age. This is when they are at their best. They are sometimes confused as unripe damsons, but the difference can be distinguished by the leaves being lighter in colour and the fruits themselves being rounded, rather than oblong in shape. In the wild they can be found growing alongside damsons in hedgerows of country lanes, woodland fringes, fields, and meadow borders.

### What To Do

Jams – Yes

Wines & Spirits – Yes

Dried Out – Yes

Herbal Teas – Yes

Pies & Crumbles – Yes

Eaten Raw – Yes

Sauces – Yes

Syrups & Cordials – Yes

53

## ☺ **Crab Apple**

*Malus sylvestris*
*Up to 10 m | October – January*

Despite the high numbers available, this fruit is seldom picked. They are similar to cultivated species of apple and contain natural pectin. Over the centuries the crab apple has been eaten by man, with many concoctions of foods, wines, and ciders being made from them. Britain has a native species, but many trees are cross-contaminated of cultivated species, which has mellowed their bitter tannins. Crab apples are best picked at their ripest, usually at the end of September, where a knock of the branch can create a shower of apples. They can be found in woodlands, hedgerows, country lane fringes, parks, and scrublands.

### What To Do

Jams – Yes

Wines & Spirits – Yes

Dried Out – Yes

Herbal Teas – Yes

Pies & Crumbles – Yes

Eaten Raw – Yes

Sauces – Yes

Syrups & Cordials – Yes

# Wild Gooseberry ☺

*Ribes uva-crispa var reclinatum*
*Up to 2 m | July – September*

Gooseberries are a classic fruit of Britain, and Staffordshire is blessed to have it growing wild. Yet you may not have noticed when you pass a gooseberry bush. The fruits have a tendency to merge into the foliage, and one may have to take a second glance to notice the hoard of fruits it hold. The gooseberry is a thorny bush, which is prized by allotment holders, but it is very often found amongst hedgerows and grows quite widespread and sometimes singularly in the limestone areas of the Peak District. It can also be found in overgrown gardens in towns and villages.

## What To Do

Jams – Yes
Wines & Spirits – Yes
Dried Out – Yes
Herbal Teas – Yes
Pies & Crumbles – Yes
Eaten Raw – Yes
Sauces – Yes
Syrups & Cordials – Yes

# Juniper ☺

*Juniperus communis*
*2 – 10 m | April – October*

The juniper is shrouded is history. During the plague days, branches were burnt by folk to ward off sickness. They have been associated with good and bad luck. However, they have many culinary uses, the biggest association with the production of gin. They can also be used for various spices. They are found usually within woodlands, heaths, and moors, and very often in limestone dales. They can also be found as ornamental trees in parks and gardens.

## What To Do

Jams – No
Wines & Spirits – Yes
Dried Out – Yes
Herbal Teas – Yes
Pies & Crumbles – No
Eaten Raw – Yes
Sauces – Yes
Syrups & Cordials – Yes

# Nuts

A seasonal delicacy that is not to be missed, nuts are an important food source because they are high in fatty acids and nutrients. In the autumn, squirrels can be seen scurrying back and forth frantically trying to build up their winter supplies. This is the best time to be looking for nuts.

All species described are found in high numbers, so foragers will feel as though they have struck gold when they come across a fresh supply of edible nuts fallen on the forest floor. They should take advantage of this, because nuts can be kept well into the winter and can be cooked in many ways.

The best and biggest nut found is the sweet chestnut. This is a delicacy that is not to be missed. Although they have a spiny husk, one or two pricks to the hands is soon forgotten when the nut is tasted.

Nuts also have the advantage of being eaten on the move when out in the field. It is highly recommended that all readers of this guide use the species described to find that highly prized hoard and to further their knowledge of excellent sources of wild foods.

# Hazel ☺

*Corylus avellana*
*2 – 7 m | September – November*

The wood from the hazel cannot be mistaken with many others. Its shoots grow straight, with thick foliage at the tops. The hazel has long been used by shepherds and walkers for walking sticks, but its nuts, which are available in the autumn, are very highly prized. Some trees yield few nuts, but most will hold thousands. However, when picking, one will not be alone; nature, particularly squirrels, also prize them for storing over winter. They are not often found amongst pine woods, but they are very common in deciduous woodlands and nutrient-rich soils. It can also be found growing in gardens, hedgerows, and country parks, sometimes as ornamental plants, but some are self-seeded due to fine pollen from its catkins, which blow in the wind during spring. It is worth noting that the catkins are also edible.

## What To Do

- The nuts can be gathered in great quantities are stored for winter use.
- The nuts can be roasted in sand in hot embers.
- The nuts can be chopped and added to salads.
- The chopped nuts can be added to chocolate for a nutty taste.
- The chopped nuts can be added to a variety of savoury dishes and roasted.
- The chopped nuts are good as part of a salad dressing oil.

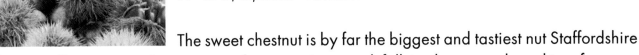

# Sweet Chestnut ☺

*Castanea sativa*
*10 – 30 m | September – November*

The sweet chestnut is by far the biggest and tastiest nut Staffordshire has to offer. During the autumn, chestnuts ripen and fall to the ground, making for easy pickings. The leaves are oblong with a pointed tip and are very hard to confuse with other tree species. The nuts themselves are encased in a spiny husk shell which can be avoided by stepping on the shell to crack it, then using two sticks to prize it open. Chestnuts are a delicacy and are sold in many stalls, particularly at Christmas. They have a sweet taste that is like no other. Other ways to cook them are straight on hot embers, in an oven, or even in the microwave – but prick them first, because they tend to explode unexpectedly. Chestnuts can be found in deciduous woodland across Staffordshire, on country road sides, in country parks, and in town and city parks.

## What To Do

- Can be used to make a chestnut chocolate.
- Can be pickled in oil for preserving.
- The chopped nuts can be added to salads or fruit salads.
- Can be eaten raw.
- Can be stored in the shells over winter and used accordingly.

## ☺ **Pines**

*Pinus*
*3 – 50 m | September – November*

The pine is by far the most successful of Staffordshire's trees. Their ability to grow in places of low light allows them to be quite versatile in the habitats they can grow. The wood is highly prized in the timber industry, and although the nuts can be quite fiddly to extract, they are very much worth the effort because they are high in fatty oils, which is very important if hungry and on the move. Pines grow all over Staffordshire; quite often entire woodlands or forests are solely pines. They can also be found on country lane borders, in parks as ornamental trees, or as barriers for children's playgrounds.

### What To Do

- The nuts can be used as part of a green pesto recipe.
- The nuts are excellent as part of salads.
- The nuts can be used for an extra crunch in curries.
- The nuts can be added to sauces.
- The finely chopped nuts can be added to desserts.

59

### What To Do

- The nuts can be eaten as a snack on the move.
- The nuts can be added to salads.
- The chopped nuts can be added to cheesecakes and other desserts.
- The chopped nuts can be added to many sauces.
- The chopped nuts can be added to salads.
- The nuts can be stored over winter months.

## ☺ **Beech**

*Fagus sylvatica*
*25 to 30 m | September – November*

The humble beech has a long history. This native tree is a giant amongst the tall. The height and spread of the branches dwarf many other trees. They can live for many centuries and are a sanctuary for many birds and squirrels. Beech tree wood is used in the timber industry as a hardwood and is very expensive. The trees themselves can yield thousands of beech nuts on one tree, many within arm's length. Although the nuts are smallish in size, they can be gathered in quantities and are very high in fatty acids. They are also excellent as a snack on the move. Beech trees can be found all over Staffordshire, mainly in deciduous woodlands and forests; they can also be found growing with pines. They are an icon tree in parks and are very common in rural areas and country parks. Some smaller species are grown as part of hedgerows. They can also be found as ornamental trees in large gardens.

60

# Fungi

Before the excitement of foraging for your own mushrooms begins, it's worth taking a minute to read these guidelines, because fungi are the most dangerous of all foods to be discussed in *The Staffordshire Larder*.

Beginners may have constant doubts in their minds about how safe wild mushrooms are. In reality, they are very safe for consumption, providing you have ALWAYS made a 100 per cent identification. A lot needs to be taken into consideration when identifying mushrooms, as so many species look similar, but some safe for consumption and some deadly. Quite often the combination of them both is found growing in the same location. There are several types of mushroom that can be identified.

**Mushrooms with pores / sponge**          **Mushrooms with gills / false gills**
**Coral fungi**          **Sac fungi**          **Jelly fungi**          **Crust fungi**
                         **Bracket fungi**      **Stinkhorns**          **Puffballs**

This guide does not identify mushrooms from each of these types; it does identify mushroom where little or no confusion is made, making it much easier for the reader to identify. In the case where a type has a close poisonous lookalike, a warning will be given.

This guide will also make points about what to look out for when trying to make an identification, as a positive ID can be made on where, when , how, and the structure of a mushroom grows, all of which will determine the mushroom it is.

- Mushrooms with gills or false gills will have a cap at the top, sometimes with remnants of the volva on (also known as the universal veil), gills underneath, and stipe (stem). Some mushrooms here will also have a ring or partial veil, almost like a curtain around the stem. At the bottom will be a volva, which is the base of the mushroom.
- Mushrooms with pores or sponge will look exactly the same as gilled mushrooms; however, instead of gills it will be a sponge or porous-like texture.
- Coral fungi are very simple in structure, being the same at the bottom as well as the top.
- Sac fungi again are quite simple in structure, often growing in cup shapes, sometimes closed (for example, truffles).
- Jelly fungi are exactly what it suggests – quite often growing on branches and looking as though jelly has been sprinkled on.
- Crust fungi grow almost similarly in texture to that of lichen.
- Bracket fungi tends to be quite hard in texture, quite often growing from trees. Most types are not edible.
- Stinkhorns are easy to identify due to their smell they omit, and they are often covered in flies. They resemble a mushroom with gills but do not contain them.
- Puffballs are simple to identify and the structure is simple. They are often just a ball, sometimes with a short stem, but the flesh inside is pure throughout with no gills. When mature the seeds burst out of the bodies, usually in a puff of smoke, hence their name.

Although many considerations must be made, mushrooms are worth picking. If one is 100 per cent positive, then try them out. If unsure, take note of its growing conditions, take a sample home, and make in-depth identifications for future reference. Further study of mycology can be made by booking courses with a professional mycologist.

# Jew's Ear /Jelly Ear / Ear Fungus ☺

*Hirneola auricular-judae*
*2 – 20 cm | All Year*

It was said that Judas Iscariot, who betrayed Jesus before his crucifixion, had hung himself on an elder tree in shame, and the Jew's ear fungus is an everlasting mark of that event. Jew's ears cannot be mistaken for any other fungi; their shape and texture is unique, not just for how it looks but also how it grows. It can be found all year round. In the summer they dry out, and through the winter seasons they fatten back out for the forager to collect. The Jew's ear grows exclusively on elder trees. If you see similar fungi on any other tree, do not collect it, because it will not be Jew's ear. Like all wild fungi, the Jew's ear should always be cooked thoroughly first. Elder trees are usually found near a water source. They can be found near river banks, large and wet gardens, brooks, woodlands, and country parks.

**What To Use For**

DRIED OUT – YES
SOUPS – YES
STEWS & CASSEROLES – YES
STIR FRYS – YES
SAUCES – YES
PASTA DISHES – YES

# Chicken of the Woods ☺

*Laetiporus sulphureus*
*1 – 5 m | April – October*

A chicken of the woods mushroom will astonish one with its size. The chicken of the woods are one of the few palatable bracket fungi, and only one specimen will suffice for the pot. In fact the fungus is actually a parasite fungus which grows on deciduous trees in lowland forests. The chicken of the woods has been confused with the cinnamon bracket; although growing in similar conditions, the cinnamon bracket is much smaller and a different colour. It can be found in all areas of Staffordshire on deciduous trees, from country park woodlands to nature reserves and valley coppices.

**What To Use For**

DRIED OUT – YES
SOUPS – YES
STEWS & CASSEROLES – YES
STIR FRYS – YES
SAUCES – YES
PASTA DISHES – NO

## ☺ **Oyster Mushroom**

*Pleurotus ostreatus*
*3 – 8 cm | September – March*

A classic and highly underestimated mushroom, the oyster mushroom can be found throughout the winter, when many other mushrooms are gone. It does have a close lookalike called the olive osysterling. The difference here is that the olive osysterling has a yellow stipe (stem) and tends to grow on fallen trees, whereas the oyster mushroom will sometimes grow off the ground, sometimes a few metres up or on tree stumps, mainly on beech. The oyster mushroom can be found all across Staffordshire in deciduous woodland, sometimes in country parks where a group of beech trees may lie.

### What To Use For

DRIED OUT – YES
SOUPS – YES
STEWS & CASSEROLES – YES
STIR FRYS – YES
SAUCES – YES
PASTA DISHES – YES

63

## ☺ **Puffballs**

*Bovista / Lycoperdon*
*3 – 8 cm | Juoly – November*

Many species of puffball exist, the largest specimen being the Giant puffball, which can grow up to half a metre across. They are edible when they are pure white inside, at their young stage, as they get older their seeds mature inside the fungi and burst out. All puffballs are edible apart from the common earthball, which grows in coniferous woodland and has a mould look and texture to it inside. (see the Ten no no's on page 76) Puffballs can be found widely in Staffordshire, from grassy meadows, to deciduous and coniferous woodland, some with no soil preference.

### What To Use For

DRIED OUT – YES
SOUPS – YES
STEWS & CASSEROLES – YES
STIR FRYS – YES
SAUCES – YES
PASTA DISHES – YES

# Amethyst Deceiver ☺

*Laccaria amethystina*
*2 – 5 cm | June – July*

This is one mushroom where you will have to get on your hands and knees to find. The amethyst deceiver has false gills and looks like no other. It is purple in colour (similar to that of lavender) and is very small; however, it is worthy of The Staffordshire Larder because its taste and smell is fantastic and makes excellent eating. It can be found in deciduous or coniferous woodland, with no soil preference, all across Staffordshire.

## What To Use For

DRIED OUT – YES
SOUPS – YES
STEWS & CASSEROLES – YES
STIR FRYS – YES
SAUCES – YES
PASTA DISHES – YES

64

# Boletus ☺

*Boletus*
*8 – 20 cm | July – November*

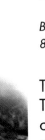

The boletus family is among the best of any mushroom to be found. They have sponge instead of gills, so little confusion is made. They can bruise easily, as indicated by black markings appearing on the sponge, so always transport with care. Only a couple specimens in the boletus family are toxic; as a rule of thumb, any specimens that have a red stem or are white in colour should be avoided. The boletus can be found all through Staffordshire, mainly in deciduous forests but occasionally in coniferous forests.

## What To Use For

DRIED OUT – YES
SOUPS – YES
STEWS & CASSEROLES – YES
STIR FRYS – YES
SAUCES – YES
PASTA DISHES – NO

# ☺ **Chanterelle**

*Cantharellus cibarius*
*3 – 10 cm | July – November*

Reputably expensive and often referred to as the best tasting wild mushroom in the world, this mushroom is very worthy of picking. It has false gills and a cap which collapses in the centre. A close lookalike, the false chanterelle, is also edible. Many people warn of another lookalike, the jack-o'-lantern, which is poisonous; however, this mainly occurs in Southern Europe and grows on dead wood. The chanterelle grows mainly in coniferous woodlands and forests and is very commonly found everywhere in Staffordshire.

## What To Use For

DRIED OUT – YES
SOUPS – YES
STEWS & CASSEROLES – YES
STIR FRYS – YES
SAUCES – YES
PASTA DISHES – YES

**66**

# Animals

Animal life is complex. When we buy our meats pre-packed from a supermarket, we accept that we don't need to worry about where the product has come from; we only eat what is offered. The human body needs protein in its diet, and in daily life we are limited with our choice. In the wild we have a larger supermarket of meats to choose from, if you know where to look and what is defined as food.

Protein sources come from the air, land, underground, and water. Birds, mammals, fish, grubs, and insects were and still are staple parts of Homo sapiens diet. In the United Kingdom our ancestors went with the seasons, winter obviously being the hardest time to find food running around.

The easiest source of animals for eating is grubs and insects. They are easily gathered, and some, like the grasshopper and various larvae of beetles, are very high in protein, sometimes more than traditional meat. Next will come animals with legs, the mammals. Finding and hunting animals in the UK is difficult. This is because stalking and trapping animals is a difficult process to master and takes practice, but also the use of primitive weapons, such as bows and arrows, is illegal. The best way to hunt for animals is by trapping, and of course by land owner's permission.

When stalking animals, it is important to mix a combination of recognising the tracks of the animal you are looking for, entering its frame of mind, and most important, patience.

67

However, other protein sources which can be found are fish and birds and the eggs they lay. Birds, like most wildlife in the UK, are protected by pieces of legislation, so once again the best way to hunt birds is from landowner permission or through organised shoots.

If you an opportunist, there is always the choice of road kill. Highly undervalued, road kill is a great free food offer. A general rule of thumb is, if it smells okay, then it's probably good for eating. Like all fresh foods, though, the best result either requires the food to be frozen to preserve the freshness, or to be eaten straight away.

Whichever your opinion on the ways to collect and use animals, it is without doubt that we need them as part of a healthy diet, and the best choice and best freshness to offer is that of what we find ourselves in the wild.

# Rabbit ☺

*Oryctolagus cuniculas*
*35 – 40 cm*

There are many reasons why you should eat rabbit. They were used extensively during the Second World War as a staple part of the diet because they were in supply, and not much has changed since then. They are still plentiful, but we do not eat them as much anymore. They are a great definition of fast food. Rabbit has been rumoured to be 99 per cent fat free and very low in cholesterol, which makes it the healthiest meat you could eat. Rabbits are in great supply in every part of the countryside throughout Staffordshire. Many farmers have problems with rabbits and so will direct most people to the quickest way to take one home. They are active at all parts of the day, but especially at dawn and dusk.

## What To Use For

| | | |
|---|---|---|
| SOUPS – YES | STEWS & CASSEROLES – YES | ROASTING – YES |
| EATEN RARE – YES | SAUCES – YES | SALADS – YES |
| SANDWICHES – YES | FROZEN – YES | |
| CONTINENTAL & INTERNATIONAL DISHES – YES | | |

# Hare ☺

*Laetiporus sulphureus*
*60 – 70 cm*

Hares are not as common as rabbit, and their numbers have declined alarmingly; however, they can still be found widespread. Hares have much longer legs than rabbits, and in spring they can infamously be seen "boxing", which is part of the males' mating ritual. Hares also have the tendency to disappear from one's eye in a wide open field, as they dig out hollows in the ground in which they crouch in to avoid being seen by predators. Hares are found in similar conditions to rabbits, throughout the Staffordshire countryside, and are active at all parts of the day. Please bear in mind the declination of the hare before venturing out in pursuit of this fantastic animal, as it may become part the endangered species list if careful consideration is not made.

## What To Use For

| | | |
|---|---|---|
| SOUPS – YES | STEWS & CASSEROLES – YES | ROASTING – YES |
| EATEN RARE – YES | SAUCES – YES | SALADS – YES |
| SANDWICHES – YES | FROZEN – YES | |
| CONTINENTAL & INTERNATIONAL DISHES – YES | | |

# ☺ **Grey Squirrel**

*Sciurus carolinensis*
*25 – 30 cm*

A classic and highly underestimated mushroom, the oyster mushroom can be found throughout the winter, when many other mushrooms are gone. It does have a close lookalike called the olive osysterling. The difference here is that the olive osysterling has a yellow stipe (stem) and tends to grow on fallen trees, whereas the oyster mushroom will sometimes grow off the ground, sometimes a few metres up or on tree stumps, mainly on beech. The oyster mushroom can be found all across Staffordshire in deciduous woodland, sometimes in country parks where a group of beech trees may lie.

## What To Use For

| | | |
|---|---|---|
| SOUPS – YES | STEWS & CASSEROLES – YES | ROASTING – YES |
| EATEN RARE – YES | SAUCES – YES | SALADS – YES |
| SANDWICHES – YES | FROZEN – YES | |
| CONTINENTAL & INTERNATIONAL DISHES – YES | | |

69

# ☺ **Land Snails**

*Capaea / Helix*
*6 – 55 mm*

Too many, snails are a last resort wild food, but treated in the right way, they can be good eating. The traditional way to prepare snails was to purge (detox) them of their impurities. The best way to do this is to collect and feed them on a diet of garlic or lettuce for four days. They are best cooked with garlic or something similar; they can also be kept alive until they are wanted for eating. Snails are very common throughout all of Staffordshire, in gardens, towns, cities, and all parts of the countryside.

## What To Use For

| | | |
|---|---|---|
| SOUPS – YES | STEWS & CASSEROLES – YES | ROASTING – YES |
| EATEN RARE – NO | SAUCES – YES | SALADS – YES |
| SANDWICHES – NO | FROZEN – NO | |
| CONTINENTAL & INTERNATIONAL DISHES – YES | | |

# Earth Worm ☺

*Lumbricus terrestris*
*Up to 8 cm*

Very abundant and also highly invaluable for the breakdown of dead matter, earthworms do not have a good reputation as an edible food, but it is easily gathered in times of emergency as a great protein source. It's always recommended to squeeze your fingers down a worm to remove its waste. A good way to make earth worms more palatable is to dry them out in the sun or oven and ground down, then add them to soups and the like. Earthworms are sensitive to vibration, which brings them to them surface and makes for easy pickings. However, they can also be easily found during wet weather and at night. Earthworms can be found throughout all of Staffordshire in most soils, both urban or rural. They are not as common in acid soils, such as peat bogs.

## What To Use For

| | | |
|---|---|---|
| SOUPS – YES | STEWS & CASSEROLES – YES | ROASTING – YES |
| EATEN RARE – YES | SAUCES – YES | SALADS – YES |
| SANDWICHES – YES | FROZEN – YES | |
| CONTINENTAL & INTERNATIONAL DISHES – YES | | |

# Grasshoppers ☺

*Myrmeleotettix/Chorthippus /Omocestus /Stenobothris / Steothphyma /Gomphoceripus*
*7 – 50 cm*

Grasshoppers are very common, especially through hot spells; if not seen, they can be heard. The noise that grasshoppers make is from their hind legs being rubbed together. Although they can jump far, they can be caught quite easily. They can be eaten raw but are best cooked. A good tip is to remove the legs because they have a tendency to get stuck in between the teeth. Grasshoppers favour meadows, but any grassland during hot periods will bring grasshoppers out. They are not usually found in urban areas or woodlands.

## What To Use For

| | | |
|---|---|---|
| SOUPS – YES | STEWS & CASSEROLES – YES | ROASTING – YES |
| EATEN RARE – NO | SAUCES – YES | SALADS – YES |
| SANDWICHES – YES | FROZEN – YES | |
| CONTINENTAL & INTERNATIONAL DISHES – YES | | |

## ☺ **Carp**

*Cyprinus carpio*
25 cm – 1 m

Recent highlight of carp has brought their culinary potential to light. Although eaten commonly in many parts of Europe, carp is not very much eaten in the United Kingdom. Repudiated to have a soil taste, they can be turn into great dishes. They can be found in canals, lakes, ponds, and reservoirs throughout Staffordshire.

### What To Use For

| | | |
|---|---|---|
| SOUPS – NO | STEWS & CASSEROLES – NO | ROASTING – YES |
| EATEN RARE – YES | SAUCES – NO | SALADS – YES |
| SANDWICHES – YES | FROZEN – YES | |
| CONTINENTAL & INTERNATIONAL DISHES – NO | | |

### What To Use For

SOUPS – YES

STEWS & CASSEROLES – NO

ROASTING – YES

EATEN RARE – NO

SAUCES – YES

SALADS – YES

SANDWICHES – YES

FROZEN – YES

CONTINENTAL & INTERNATIONAL DISHES – YES

## ☺ **Signal Crayfish**

*Astacus pallipes*
Up to 60 cm

Not to be confused with the native species, the American signal crayfish has caused many problems throughout UK waterways. They are named after their reddened underside of the claws, which they happily flash to show their defences. The signal is much larger than the native crayfish and has been known to cause disease. They are classed as vermin and can be caught easily. Some ways to catch signal crayfish are to fish or catch in a baited basket. However, the easiest way to catch is to turn over rocks in shallow, slow-flowing water. Then it's just a case of sneaking up on the crayfish. They can be collected in great quantities and are great eating. The most humane way to dispatch them is to freeze. It is also worth noting that the spine must be removed before cooking; this is found on the middle part of the tail. To remove, snap one way then the other, then pull out. They can be found in most rivers throughout Staffordshire but are also in feeds and canal systems.

# Freshwater Snails ☺

*Lymnaea stagnalis*
*6 – 45 mm*

Found in various sizes, the freshwater snail is a silent creature living quite commonly in Staffordshire's waterways. They can be treated similarly to land snails, and it is recommended that purging is done before eating to remove impurities. Freshwater snails favour ponds but can be found in lakes, rivers, and canals all across Staffordshire.

## What To Use For

SOUPS – YES          STEWS & CASSEROLES – YES          ROASTING – YES
EATEN RARE – NO      SAUCES – YES                       SALADS – YES
SANDWICHES – YES     FROZEN – NO
CONTINENTAL & INTERNATIONAL DISHES – YES

72

# Freshwater Clams / Swan Mussel ☺

*Anodonta cygnea*
*Up to 12 cm*

The freshwater clam is an impressive creature which is not very often seen, and it could become endangered if careful consideration is not made. Despite this, the swan mussel is relatively common. At times of drought, empty shells can be seen littered in the mud of lakes and reservoirs. They can be treated like mussels found on the coast. Freshwater clams can be found in canals, reservoirs, and lakes throughout Staffordshire.

## What To Use For

SOUPS – YES          STEWS & CASSEROLES – NO          ROASTING – NO
EATEN RARE – NO      SAUCES – YES                      SALADS – YES
SANDWICHES – NO      FROZEN – NO
CONTINENTAL & INTERNATIONAL DISHES – YES

## ☺ **Red Deer**

*Cervus elaphus*
*1 – 1.5 m in height*

A greatly impressive mammal and the largest in the United Kingdom. Many specimens exist in Staffordshire, but their ability to disappear in a blink of an eye is bewildering. To track and find these animals is greatly rewarding, and the meat from them is greatly prized. Please be aware, though, that shooting without landowners' permission is illegal. Red deer can be found in pockets of woodland and forests on the fringes of towns and villages, and throughout the Peak District.

### What To Use For

SOUPS – YES          STEWS & CASSEROLES – YES          ROASTING – YES
EATEN RARE – YES     SAUCES – YES                      SALADS – YES
SANDWICHES – YES     FROZEN – YES
CONTINENTAL & INTERNATIONAL DISHES – YES

## ☺ **Mallard**

*Anas platyrhynchos*
*50 – 65 cm*

A very common duck. Many families associate feeding the ducks specifically with mallards. The male mallard is the more colourful sex; the female is brown in colour. Often they can be seen in pairs; however, it's also common to see many male mallards together. Mallards are very good eating, but quite often landowner permission is needed before shooting these ducks. Mallards can be found everywhere in Staffordshire, where water may be present, from ponds to lakes, reservoirs, canals, town parks, and any other waterways.

### What To Use For

SOUPS – YES          STEWS & CASSEROLES – YES          ROASTING – YES
EATEN RARE – YES     SAUCES – YES                      SALADS – YES
SANDWICHES – YES     FROZEN – YES
CONTINENTAL & INTERNATIONAL DISHES – YES

# Pheasant ☺

*Phasianus colchicus*
*50 – 60 cm*

By far one of the most common game birds, pheasants were originally imported from Asia but soon dominated the British Wildlife. Pheasants are fantastic eating. Traditionally gamekeepers allow shoots on their lands, but pheasants also are a great road kill contender. They can be found throughout the Staffordshire's countryside, country parks, and the Moorlands.

## What To Use For

| | | |
|---|---|---|
| SOUPS – YES | STEWS & CASSEROLES – YES | ROASTING – YES |
| EATEN RARE – YES | SAUCES – YES | SALADS – YES |
| SANDWICHES – YES | FROZEN – YES | |
| CONTINENTAL & INTERNATIONAL DISHES – YES | | |

74

# Red Grouse ☺

*Lagopus lagopus*
*30 – 45 cm*

Yet another game bird, the red grouse is very much worthy of The Staffordshire Larder for its great eating. Although only found on the Moorlands, it can sometimes be found as road kill. Most areas for shooting on the Moorlands are owned by various people that organise shoots for grouse during the shooting season. It is highly recommended to ask permission before.

## What To Use For

| | | |
|---|---|---|
| SOUPS – YES | STEWS & CASSEROLES – YES | ROASTING – YES |
| EATEN RARE – YES | SAUCES – YES | SALADS – YES |
| SANDWICHES – YES | FROZEN – YES | |
| CONTINENTAL & INTERNATIONAL DISHES – YES | | |

# ☺ **Wood Pigeon**

*Columba palumbus*
*Up to 45 cm*

Wood pigeons are extremely common and have a bad habit of flying away long before you get there. They are plump to look at and are notoriously shy. Unless specifically hunting for them, it is very hard and uncommon to be lucky enough to catch one. The best part to eat is the breast meat, which makes fantastic eating. They can be found in any rural or urban location throughout all of Staffordshire.

## What To Use For

SOUPS – YES          STEWS & CASSEROLES – YES          ROASTING – YES
EATEN RARE – YES     SAUCES – YES                      SALADS – YES
SANDWICHES – YES     FROZEN – YES
CONTINENTAL & INTERNATIONAL DISHES – YES

75

# ☺ **Trout**

*Salmo trutta*
*40 – 70 cm*

Trout are no doubt the best of Staffordshire's fish; they are great eating and are satisfying to catch. Trout have a long history through game fishers, to the point that specialist trout farms can be found dotted around the county. Many rivers where trout are found are owned by various people, and catching fish in these areas is illegal without landowners' permission first. However, they are worth the wait because they can be made into many fine culinary dishes. Trout can be found in freshwater and non-polluted rivers throughout Staffordshire. They are also in shallow rivers, sheltering under tree roots or large boulders.

## What To Use For

SOUPS – YES          STEWS & CASSEROLES – YES          ROASTING – YES
EATEN RARE – NO      SAUCES – YES                      SALADS – YES
SANDWICHES – NO      FROZEN – NO
CONTINENTAL & INTERNATIONAL DISHES – YES

# Ten No-Nos

Below is a list of ten simple rules and myths to remember when foraging for wild foods, so as to not turn your food hunt into a trip to the hospital.

### Age Before Beauty

It's a well-known fact that as plants and fungi age they release toxins. Many plants will look their prettiest just as they are at their height of growth, but for the best pickings a good guideline is to pick only the younger specimens.

### Beware the Earthballs

The earthball, a member of the puffball family, is the only toxic one. They are recognisable from their pimpled, pigskin beige colour, and the texture inside resembles the charred remains of a fire. They are deadly, so avoid at all costs.

### Horseradish or Dockleaf

So which do you think it is? Dockleafs are recognisable by their red colourisation on the leaves when they mature, as well as the seeds appearing. If you are unsure still, pick the root and rub your fingernail over it. It should have a strong horseradish smell; then you know you've got the right one.

### Bigger Is Not Better

Some of the tastiest wild foods are the smallest. The amethyst deceiver mushroom, chickweed, and ant larvae are all very tasty and all very small.

### Too Much of Something Can Be Bad for the Health

It is easy to get carried away with picking many of the same species, especially if they are berries. However, too much of one species can cause upset stomach, so always limited yourself to small quantities.

### Always Be 100 Per Cent Positive

Whichever species you plan to take, always ensure that you have the right one. Many people have landed in hospital from eating something and were unaware of its poisonous outcome.

### Take Only What You Need

As mentioned previously, you must always be considerate in taking wild foods. Remember that you are not alone in eating wild foods, as nature relies on it. Also be considerate to others who are also looking for the same species.

### Never Cause Any Unnecessary Damage

When foraging for wild foods, be careful about causing damage to local flora and fauna. Your actions can easily destroy a habitat.

77

### Beware the Bright Colours

Some species display bright colours to alert that they are poisonous. Unless it's described in this guide, or you're 100 per cent positive, leave it alone, as the chances are that it is poisonous.

### Respect Is the Best Attitude

Consideration is paramount. Don't forget you are entering the homes of native species when picking them, and you must always respect this. Don't drop your litter, keep noise down, and follow the countryside code so that future generations can enjoy the benefits of wild food as well.

# The Top Ten

1     **Nettle** – By far the best plant to be found in Staffordshire. It is found from early in the year, is gathered easily enough, and has many uses. *see page 18*

2     **Rabbit** – A fantastic food. Plentiful in supply, low in fat, versatile, and great eating. You just have to catch them. *see page 68*

3     **Blackberry** – A summer classic. Hoards appear in late summer and into autumn, and they have many uses. *see page 50*

4     **Crayfish** – The mini lobster. So many plague the rivers that it is too good to miss the opportunity of a free, expensive meal. *see page 71*

5     **Chickweed** – It's amazing how this plant has not got into our supermarkets, with its taste like lettuce; it is a perfect salad contender. *see page 21*

78   6     **Sweet Chestnut** – The perfect nut to eat on the go, sweet tasting and a great culinary potential. It's just a matter of getting into them. *see page 58*

7     **Boletus** – A definite continental choice, as they are picked on family outings, like blackberries in the UK. They have plenty of uses and can be stored and dried for months. *see page 64*

8     **Rosehips** – Plenty of history, and for good reason. Rosehips are exceptionally high in vitamin C and can be used in many ways. *see page 29*

9     **Wild Garlic** – A seasonal delight to keep the vampires away. Many uses and very good for the immune system. *see page 22*

10     **Mints** – Freshness and many varieties make this plant highly recommended. *see page 28*

CPSIA information can be obtained
at www.ICGtesting.com
Printed in the USA
LVIW020837210512

2835LVUK00006B